BASKETBALL'S GREAT PLAYERS

MEGAN COOLEY PETERSON

BLACK
RABBIT
BOOKS

Bolt is published by Black Rabbit Books
P.O. Box 3263, Mankato, Minnesota, 56002.
www.blackrabbitbooks.com
Copyright © 2017 Black Rabbit Books

Design and Production by Michael Sellner
Photo Research by Rhonda Milbrett

Library of Congress Control Number: 2015954672

HC ISBN: 978-1-68072-059-4   PB ISBN: 978-1-68072-265-9

Printed in the United States at CG Book Printers,
North Mankato, Minnesota, 56003. PO #1791 4/16

BOLT

CONTENTS

CHAPTER 1

On the COURT

A basketball player drives toward the basket. Jumping into the air, the player dunks the ball. The crowd roars.

Basketball's great players leave it all on the court. Flip the page, and see where your favorite players rank.

NBA BACKBOARDS

72 INCHES
(1.8 meters)

24 INCHES
(.6 m)

48 INCHES
(1.2 m)

18 INCHES
(.5 m)

TARGET AREA

BASKETBALL RIM

CHAPTER 2

The PLAYERS

Kareem Abdul-Jabbar
played from 1969–1989

Kareem Abdul-Jabbar was a scoring machine. No basketball player has scored more points. He won Most Valuable Player (MVP) six times. He also won six **NBA** championships.

24.6 AVERAGE POINTS PER GAME

38,387 CAREER POINTS

72.1% CAREER FREE THROW PERCENTAGE

11.2 AVERAGE Rebounds PER GAME

7

FREE-THROW LINE

15 FEET
(5 m)

CIRCUMFERENCE
29.5 INCHES
(75 centimeters)

WEIGHT
22 OUNCES
(624 GRAMS)

NBA
BASKETBALLS

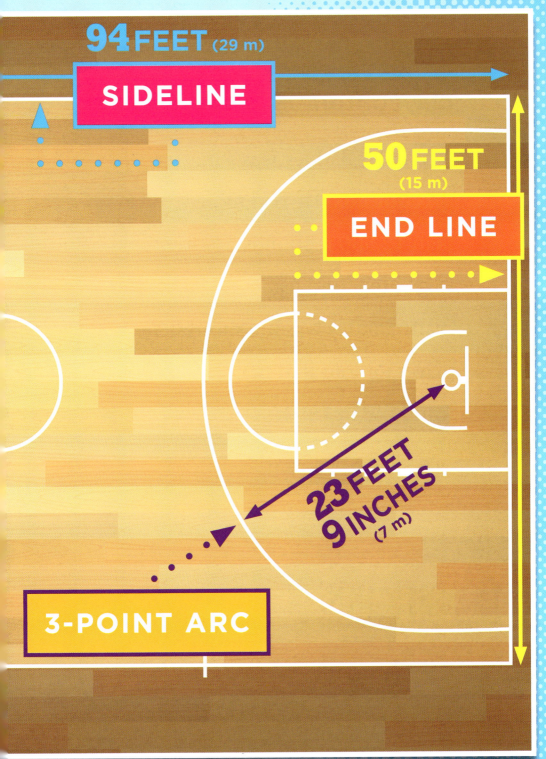

94 FEET (29 m)

SIDELINE

50 FEET (15 m)

END LINE

23 FEET **9** INCHES (7 m)

3-POINT ARC

Charles Barkley
played from 1984–2000

Charles Barkley was a master at **rebounds**. He had more than 12,500 rebounds. He was league rebound leader for three years. Barkley was the shortest player to hold that title. He also won MVP in 1993.

RANK IT!

22.1 AVERAGE POINTS PER GAME

23,757 CAREER POINTS

73.5% CAREER FREE THROW PERCENTAGE

11.7 AVERAGE Rebounds PER GAME

Wilt Chamberlain
played from 1959–1973

On March 2, 1962, Wilt Chamberlain made history. He scored 100 points in a game. "Wilt the Stilt" won MVP four times. He also holds the record for most rebounds.

RANK IT!

31,419
CAREER POINTS

30.1
AVERAGE POINTS PER GAME

51.1%
CAREER
FREE THROW
PERCENTAGE

22.9
AVERAGE REBOUNDS
PER GAME

Larry Bird
played from 1979–1992

Larry Bird could pass, score, and rebound. He practiced shooting baskets with his eyes closed. Bird led the Celtics to three championships. He also won MVP three times.

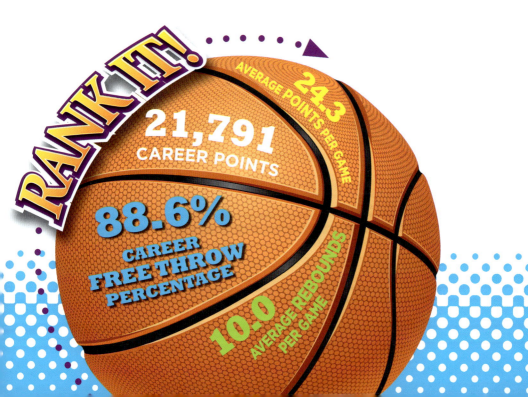

RANK IT!

24.3 AVERAGE POINTS PER GAME

21,791 CAREER POINTS

88.6% CAREER FREE THROW PERCENTAGE

10.0 AVERAGE REBOUNDS PER GAME

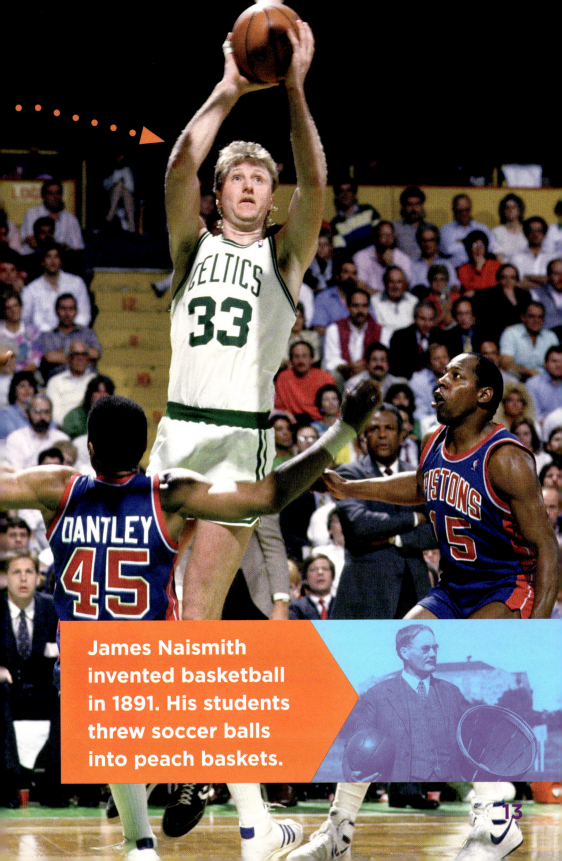

James Naismith invented basketball in 1891. His students threw soccer balls into peach baskets.

BASKETBALL TICKET

BASKETBALL'S GREAT PLAYERS

14

Cynthia Cooper
played from 1997–2003

Cynthia Cooper was the first **WNBA** superstar. She led the league in points. Cooper also helped the Comets win four championships. She became the first WNBA player to win MVP. In 1988, Cooper won an Olympic gold medal.

RANK IT!

21.0 AVERAGE POINTS PER GAME

2,601 CAREER POINTS

87.1% CAREER FREE THROW PERCENTAGE

3.20 AVERAGE Rebounds PER GAME

Kobe Bryant
played from 1996–2016

Kobe Bryant joined the NBA right after high school. He was the first Lakers player to skip college. Bryant helped his team win five championships. He also played basketball in the Olympics. Bryant won two gold medals with Team USA.

RANK IT!

25.4 AVERAGE POINTS PER GAME

32,482 CAREER POINTS

83.7% CAREER FREE THROW PERCENTAGE

5.30 AVERAGE Rebounds PER GAME

(through 2014-2015 season)

LeBron James
played from 2003–present

LeBron James blazed into the NBA after high school. He wows fans with his **blocks** and dunks. He practices shooting from the half-court line. James won **Rookie** of the Year and four MVPs. He has also won two championships so far.

RANK IT!

24,913
CAREER POINTS

27.3
AVERAGE POINTS PER GAME

74.5%
CAREER FREE THROW PERCENTAGE

7.1
AVERAGE REBOUNDS PER GAME

(through 2014-2015 season)

Michael Jordan

played between 1984 and 2003

Michael Jordan amazed fans with his daring plays. He could jump 4 feet (1 m) into the air! Jordan flew over other players when dunking.

Jordan won six championships with the Chicago Bulls. He also won five MVPs. Many people call Jordan the best player of all time.

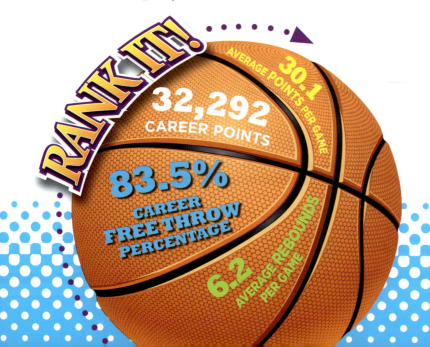

RANK IT!

32,292 CAREER POINTS

30.1 AVERAGE POINTS PER GAME

83.5% CAREER FREE THROW PERCENTAGE

6.2 AVERAGE REBOUNDS PER GAME

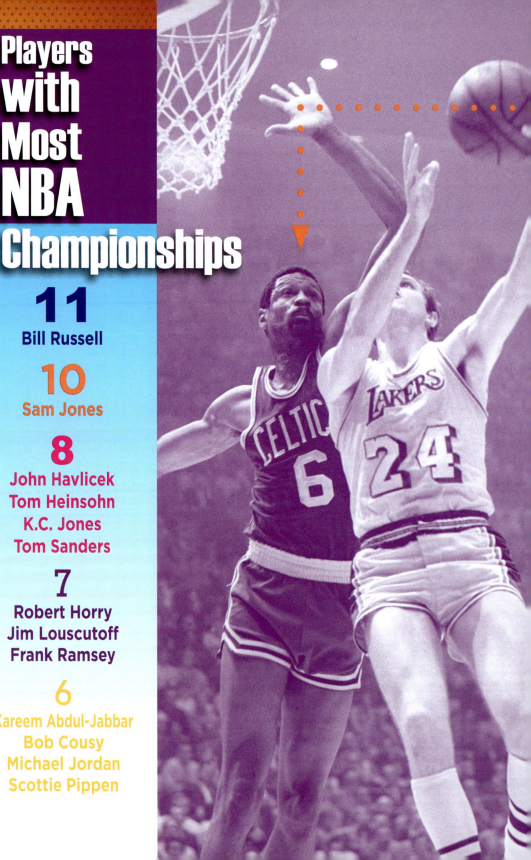

Players with Most NBA Championships

11
Bill Russell

10
Sam Jones

8
John Havlicek
Tom Heinsohn
K.C. Jones
Tom Sanders

7
Robert Horry
Jim Louscutoff
Frank Ramsey

6
Kareem Abdul-Jabbar
Bob Cousy
Michael Jordan
Scottie Pippen

• • • • Bill Russell

played from 1956–1969

Bill Russell shook up the NBA with his **defensive** plays. He blocked shots and grabbed rebounds. He led the league in rebounds four times.

Russell won five MVP awards. He also won 11 NBA championships. No other basketball player has won as many titles.

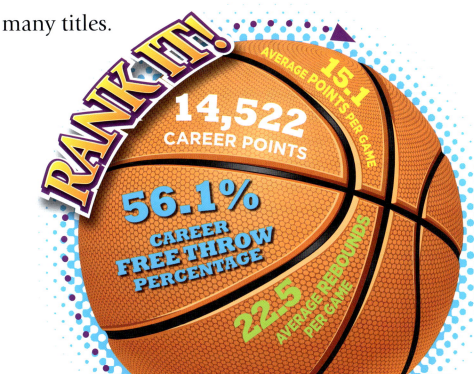

RANK IT!

15.1 AVERAGE POINTS PER GAME

14,522 CAREER POINTS

56.1% CAREER FREE THROW PERCENTAGE

22.5 AVERAGE REBOUNDS PER GAME

Magic Johnson • • • • • • • • • • •
played between 1979 and 1996

Earvin "Magic" Johnson had a magic touch when passing. His **assists** helped his teammates score. Johnson won MVP three times. At one time, he also held the record for most assists.

RANK IT!

19.5 AVERAGE POINTS PER GAME

17,707 CAREER POINTS

84.8% CAREER FREE THROW PERCENTAGE

7.20 AVERAGE Rebounds PER GAME

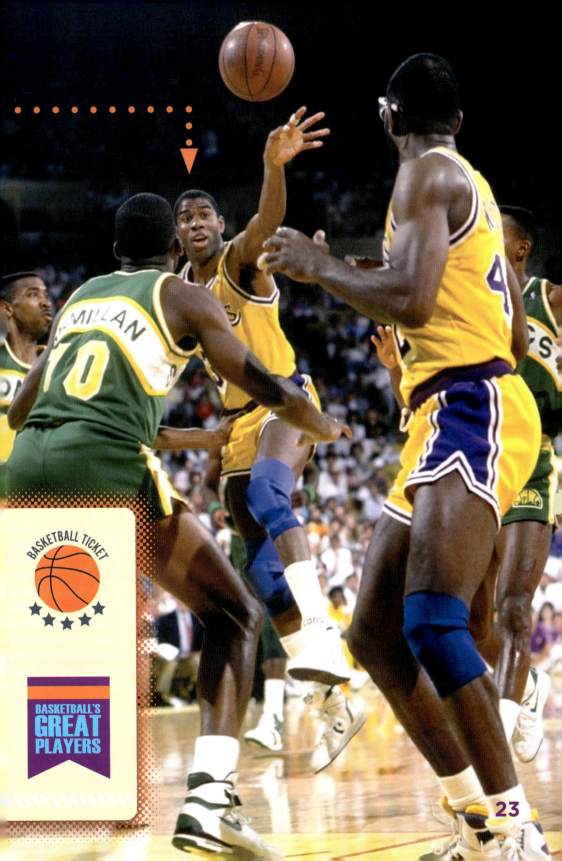

THE TALL AND SHORT OF IT

7'2"

6'10"

6'6"

6'2"

5'10"

5'6"

5'2"

5'10"
(1.77 m)

6'6"
(1.98 m)

6'6"
(1.98 m)

6'6"
(1.98 m)

6'8"
(2.03 m)

Cynthia Cooper

Charles Barkley

Kobe Bryant

Michael Jordan

LeBron James

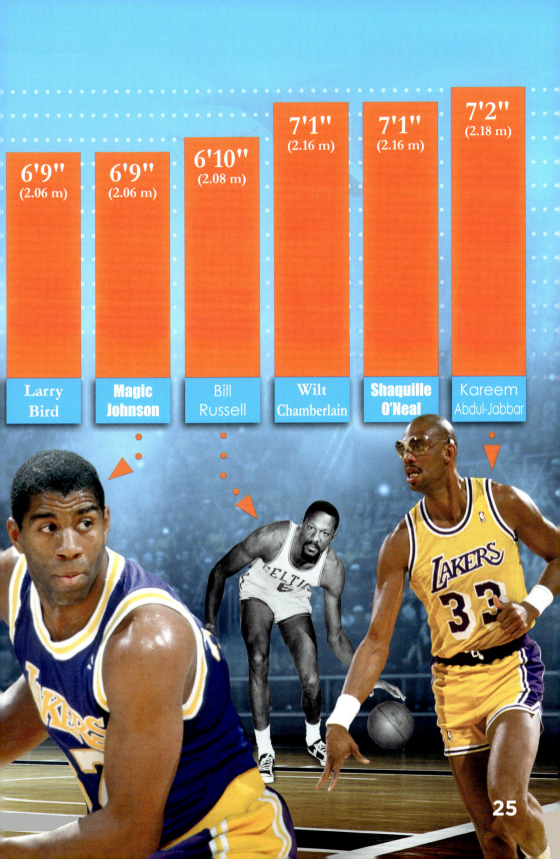

6'9"
(2.06 m)

Larry
Bird

6'9"
(2.06 m)

Magic
Johnson

6'10"
(2.08 m)

Bill
Russell

7'1"
(2.16 m)

Wilt
Chamberlain

7'1"
(2.16 m)

Shaquille
O'Neal

7'2"
(2.18 m)

Kareem
Abdul-Jabbar

Shaquille O'Neal
played from 1992–2011

Shaquille O'Neal blasted past other players. His size made him hard to stop. Other players **fouled** him to stop him from scoring.

Known as "Shaq," he won Rookie of the Year. He led the Lakers to three championships. He also won a championship with the Miami Heat.

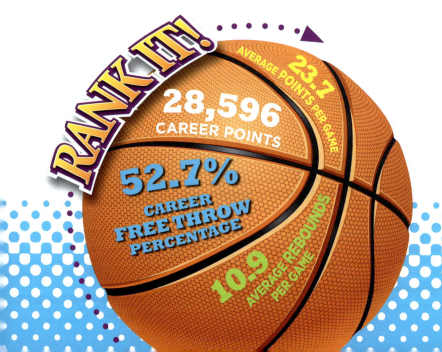

RANK IT!

AVERAGE POINTS PER GAME 23.7

28,596 CAREER POINTS

52.7% CAREER FREE THROW PERCENTAGE

10.9 AVERAGE REBOUNDS PER GAME

CHAPTER 3

Career Points

38,387	32,482*	32,292	31,419	28,596
Kareem Abdul-Jabbar	Kobe Bryant	Michael Jordan	Wilt Chamberlain	Shaquill O'Neal

BASKETBALL TICKET

BASKETBALL'S GREAT PLAYERS

Average Points Per Game

30.1	WILT CHAMBERLAIN
30.1	MICHAEL JORDAN
27.3	LEBRON JAMES*

RANK IT!

Check out how the greats stack up.

*as of 2014-2015 season

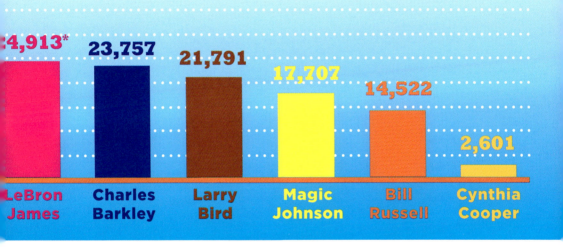

4,913*	23,757	21,791	17,707	14,522	2,601
LeBron James	Charles Barkley	Larry Bird	Magic Johnson	Bill Russell	Cynthia Cooper

AVERAGE Rebounds PER GAME

22.9 Wilt Chamberlain	22.5 Bill Russell	11.7 Charles Barkley

Career Free-Throw Percentage

88.6%	87.1%	84.8%
Larry Bird	Cynthia Cooper	Magic Johnson

GLOSSARY

assist (uh-SIST)—a pass that leads to a score by a teammate

block (BLAHK)—stopping or slowing the movement of a player or ball in a sport

defensive (de-FEN-civ)—relating to the attempt to keep someone from scoring in a game

foul (FAWL)— to do an action in basketball that is against the rules; pushing and tripping are fouls.

NBA—National Basketball Association; the NBA is a league of professional male basketball teams.

rebound (RE-bownd)—to take possession of the ball after it bounces off the backboard or rim

rookie (ROOK-ee)—a first-year player

WNBA—Women's National Basketball Association; the WNBA is a league of professional female basketball teams.

BOOKS

Abdul-Jabbar, Kareem. *Sasquatch in the Paint.* Streetball Crew. New York: Disney-Hyperion Books, 2013.

Bodden, Valerie. *Basketball.* Making the Play. Mankato, MN: Creative Education, 2016.

Sports Illustrated Kids Magazine, ed. *Sports Illustrated Kids Slam Dunk: The Top 10 of Everything in Basketball.* New York: Time Home Entertainment Inc., 2014.

WEBSITES

NBA
www.nba.com

Olympic Basketball
www.olympic.org/basketball

WNBA
www.wnba.com

INDEX